Original title:
The Calling Sky

Copyright © 2024 Swan Charm
All rights reserved.

Author: Sabrina Sarvik
ISBN HARDBACK: 978-9908-1-2281-6
ISBN PAPERBACK: 978-9908-1-2282-3
ISBN EBOOK: 978-9908-1-2283-0

The Serenade of Twinkling Lights

Underneath the starlit sky,
Laughter dances, spirits fly.
Candles flicker, joy ignites,
We gather close, on festive nights.

Strings of color, bright and bold,
Whispers of joy in tales retold.
Hearts aglow with warmth and cheer,
In this moment, love is near.

Dawn's Promise in the Heavens

Morning breaks with colors true,
A canvas spread for me and you.
Golden rays and silver sheen,
Awakening the world, so keen.

Joyful songs in the air,
Promises linger everywhere.
Children laughing, spirits lift,
In dawn's embrace, our sweetest gift.

Through the Veil of Twilight

As daylight fades and stars appear,
A hush of wonder fills the sphere.
Cool breezes sing a gentle tune,
Magic blossoms under the moon.

Lanterns glow, a soft parade,
Each flicker, dreams serenade.
Together we dance, hearts entwined,
In twilight's grasp, bliss we find.

Celestial Pathways Awaken

Comets streak across the night,
Guiding us with their bright light.
In joy and laughter, we unite,
A cosmic bond, pure and bright.

With each step, the stars align,
In every heartbeat, love will shine.
A festive glow, a sacred song,
In celestial paths, we all belong.

Evenings Under the Starry Vault

Beneath the sky where the stars ignite,
Laughter dances in the cool, soft night.
Friends gathered round with stories to share,
A magical glow fills the crisp night air.

Candles flicker in a gentle breeze,
Whispers of secrets, hearts at ease.
The moon wears silver, casting moonlit beams,
While dreams intertwine in playful schemes.

Sipping sweet cider, toasting delight,
As constellations twinkle, warm and bright.
Joy paints the evening, cheers fill the space,
In this festival charm, we find our grace.

Together we bask in the starlit glow,
Wishing for magic, letting love flow.
These evenings, a treasure, we hold so dear,
Awash in the joy, surrounded by cheer.

Celestial Dreams on a Canvas of Time

In twilight's embrace, dreams take flight,
Colors of dusk blend with soft twilight.
Brushstrokes of laughter, painting the scene,
The canvas unfolds with moments serene.

Stars like confetti scatter the sky,
With wishes and hopes, they gently pry.
The night hums a tune, sweet and low,
Echoing secrets that only we know.

Chasing the whispers of dusk's gentle sigh,
We soar through the cosmos, you and I.
With hearts as our compass, we venture wide,
In this festive dream, let our spirits glide.

Time dances softly on this painted night,
Every stroke of joy, every shimmer of light.
Together we'll wander through galaxies bright,
In celestial dreams, our hearts take flight.

Mosaics of the Ethereal Passages

Fragments of stardust, scattered and free,
We weave our stories, a tapestry.
Colors of laughter blend with each cheer,
Creating a mosaic that draws us near.

The music of joy fills the shimmering air,
As voices unite in this wondrous affair.
Each note a reminder of love's gentle touch,
In this festive gathering, it means so much.

Shadows of memories twirl in the night,
Dancing with echoes, feeling just right.
We share in the warmth of a radiant glow,
Mosaics of moments that continue to grow.

Together we laugh, together we sing,
In the embrace of the joy that we bring.
And as each hour unfolds in delight,
We craft our own magic, igniting the night.

Hanging Lanterns of Distant Worlds

Lanterns alight, glowing like dreams,
Illuminating whispers, laughter, and schemes.
A tapestry woven with magic and cheer,
Hanging like stories, both far and near.

Each flickering flame tells a tale of its own,
Of memories cherished and love that has grown.
In distant worlds, where adventures await,
We find our joy, we create our fate.

Beneath the stars, a canvas so vast,
We gather our hopes, reliving the past.
With each lantern raised, our spirits ignite,
Celebrating dreams on this festive night.

Hand in hand, we walk through the dark,
Sharing our wishes, each one a spark.
Together we shine, guided by light,
In hanging lanterns, our hearts take flight.

Celestial Summon

Stars twinkle like scattered jewels,
The night bursts with joyous light.
Gathered hearts in harmony,
Underneath the moon so bright.

Laughter sparkles in the air,
As wishes take to flight above.
Each whisper a gentle prayer,
In this realm of dreams and love.

Chasing shadows, we unite,
In this dance of endless bliss.
The universe echoes our delight,
In each moment, a perfect kiss.

Celestial calls, our spirits soar,
In a festival of gleaming night.
Together we'll forever explore,
With joy leading us to new heights.

Hanging Lanterns of Distant Worlds

Lanterns alight, glowing like dreams,
Illuminating whispers, laughter, and schemes.
A tapestry woven with magic and cheer,
Hanging like stories, both far and near.

Each flickering flame tells a tale of its own,
Of memories cherished and love that has grown.
In distant worlds, where adventures await,
We find our joy, we create our fate.

Beneath the stars, a canvas so vast,
We gather our hopes, reliving the past.
With each lantern raised, our spirits ignite,
Celebrating dreams on this festive night.

Hand in hand, we walk through the dark,
Sharing our wishes, each one a spark.
Together we shine, guided by light,
In hanging lanterns, our hearts take flight.

Celestial Summon

Stars twinkle like scattered jewels,
The night bursts with joyous light.
Gathered hearts in harmony,
Underneath the moon so bright.

Laughter sparkles in the air,
As wishes take to flight above.
Each whisper a gentle prayer,
In this realm of dreams and love.

Chasing shadows, we unite,
In this dance of endless bliss.
The universe echoes our delight,
In each moment, a perfect kiss.

Celestial calls, our spirits soar,
In a festival of gleaming night.
Together we'll forever explore,
With joy leading us to new heights.

Winds of Lunar Dreams

Gentle breezes softly swell,
Carrying tales from afar.
Moonbeams dance, cast a spell,
Lighting paths to every star.

Whispers of laughter hang in air,
As night reveals its shimmering grace.
Under the sky, we drift without care,
In this sacred, enchanted space.

Stars align, our wishes soar,
Breathing in the magic we find.
Each heartbeat a rhythm, a roar,
In the winds of dreams intertwined.

With each night, new stories unfold,
In the embrace of lunar glow.
Hand in hand, brave and bold,
We revel in this cosmic flow.

Radiance of the Twilight Realm

Golden hues touch the horizon,
As twilight unfurls its wings.
Embers of day gently wane,
While the night softly sings.

Silhouettes dance on fading light,
In the warmth of a gleaming shade.
Echoes of joy fill the night,
In this dreamy masquerade.

With laughter aloft on the breeze,
Flickers of fire ignite the sky.
Hearts in beats, we move with ease,
In the twilight where dreams lie.

Radiance shines from within,
As stars awaken, setting free.
The magic of dusk begins,
In this realm, forever we'll be.

Beneath the Aurora's Dance

Colors swirl, a vibrant display,
Painting skies with emerald light.
Underneath the aurora's sway,
We gather to share this night.

With every flicker, our spirits leap,
Floating dreams on a gentle breeze.
In this moment, our hearts will keep,
Memories sweet as honeyed bees.

Glistening stars watch from above,
As we twirl in the cosmic glow.
A celebration of life and love,
In the magic that ebbs and flows.

Beneath the aurora's guiding light,
We find our place in the vast expanse.
Together, enchanted by the night,
In this paradise, we take our chance.

Colors of Cosmic Reflection

Stars shimmer bright in the night,
Painting dreams in hues of light.
Joyful whispers fill the air,
As laughter dances everywhere.

Galaxies twirl in a grand display,
Every shadow finds its play.
Colors blend in harmony,
Creating a festive symphony.

The moon drapes silver across the land,
With gentle touch, it takes a stand.
Children gaze with wonder wide,
In cosmic beauty, hearts collide.

Together we share this lively sight,
Eternal magic, pure delight.
In this moment, hope takes flight,
Under stars, our spirits ignite.

Celestial Bridges of Hope

Across the sky, a path unfolds,
In shimmering gold, the story told.
Each star a wish, a heartfelt prayer,
Connecting souls with love and care.

With laughter echoing through the night,
We build our dreams, our hearts alight.
Celestial beams guide our way,
Lighting the night, igniting the day.

Hope flows like a river wide,
Uniting us, hearts open wide.
With every twinkling, every glance,
We celebrate in this cosmic dance.

Embrace the joy, let spirits soar,
In this festive night, there's so much more.
Together we flow like a gentle stream,
In cosmic unity, we find our dream.

A Dance Above the Earth

Underneath the starlit dome,
We gather here, far from home.
In rhythm with the moonlit glow,
Through the night, our spirits flow.

Galactic twirls and playful spins,
In our hearts, the laughter begins.
Shadows leap in silvery light,
As we dance beneath the night.

With every turn, a joy ignites,
In this magic, the world unites.
Feel the beat of joyous cheer,
As we celebrate, hold love near.

Together we sway, lost in glee,
In this moment, we are free.
A dance above, our spirits high,
Under the vast and open sky.

Tide of the Midnight Sky

Waves of stars in midnight's tide,
Whispers of dreams, our hearts abide.
Gazing up, our hopes ignite,
In a sea of wonder, pure delight.

The night unfolds a vibrant show,
As joy cascades in a silvery flow.
Each flicker brings a spark divine,
Woven together, our spirits align.

In the cool air, laughter rings,
As we celebrate the joy that brings.
Ride the tide where dreams collide,
On this wave of cosmic pride.

Together we dive in the dreamy sea,
Where the universe sings in harmony.
Tide of the sky, let us embrace,
In the heart of night, find our place.

Shadow and Light in Heavenly Vastness

In the night's embrace, stars do twinkle,
A dance of shadows, where dreams sprinkle.
Bright comets glide, their tails aglow,
While the moon whispers secrets, soft and slow.

Echoes of laughter, in twilight's grace,
Every heartbeat finds its sacred place.
Colors collide, in a celestial spree,
Nature rejoices, wild and free.

Embrace of Cosmic Currents

Waves of starlight pulse through the dark,
Crafting a melody, a celestial spark.
Planets spin gently, in a cosmic waltz,
While galaxies swirl, in a radiant pulse.

All around, the universe sings,
Whispers of joy on ethereal wings.
Tides of creation rise and fall,
In the heart of the dance, we hear the call.

The Dance of Heavenly Bodies

The sun weaves gold through the azure skies,
While stardust glimmers in children's eyes.
Saturn's rings spin in a graceful arc,
A ballet of beauty that ignites the spark.

Stars collide in a noble embrace,
Creating new worlds with effortless grace.
Each twirl, a promise, a chance to renew,
In the arms of the cosmos, forever true.

Beneath the Vast Expanse

In the hush of twilight, dreams take flight,
  Colorful lanterns dance, pure delight.
  Beneath the expanse, our spirits soar,
  As constellations weave tales of yore.

With laughter as music, hearts intertwine,
  Tracing the stardust, spirits align.
  Hand in hand, we embrace the night,
In the festive glow, everything feels right.

Out beyond the Blushing Verge

Where laughter fills the air in whirl,
The heart dances, bright, like a pearl.
Colors bloom, the joy ignites,
In a world alive with sparkling lights.

Waves of cheer with each embrace,
Smiles weave through this sacred space.
Voices rise, a merry song,
Underneath the stars, we all belong.

Dreams unfurl like ribbons wide,
In friendship's warmth, we take our stride.
Together, we chase the setting sun,
As dusk settles, our hearts beat as one.

So gather 'round, let spirits soar,
For in this union, we long for more.
With every toast, our hearts align,
In joy, we revel, intertwined.

In Hues of Nighthawk's Flight

In twilight's glow, we take to air,
As shadows blend, we share a prayer.
The night sky blooms with colors bright,
Every heart dances, pure delight.

Whispers float on gentle breeze,
With every moment, our worries cease.
Stars twinkle in the velvety dark,
Guiding us with their shimmering spark.

Stories told in laughter's embrace,
Each memory woven, a cherished lace.
Nighthawks swoop in graceful flight,
We celebrate under the moonlight.

So raise your glass to love and cheer,
In this festive night, all hold dear.
With every heartbeat, joy takes flight,
In hues alive, we're wrapped so tight.

Beneath a Canopy of Wonder

Under leaves where dreams might grow,
Laughter dances, soft and low.
Beneath this magic, we gather near,
In every glance, the world is sheer.

A tapestry of voices blend,
With every song, our hearts transcend.
The air is sweet with playful songs,
Each note a bond where we belong.

Lanterns flicker, casting glow,
In this wonder, our spirits flow.
Joy unites us, hand in hand,
Beneath the stars, together we stand.

So pause awhile, let moments freeze,
In shared delight, we're granted ease.
Underneath this canopy bright,
We find our peace, alive with light.

Celestial Pulses

Stars pulse gently through the night,
In rhythms soft, a heart takes flight.
Each beat a promise, a vibrant thread,
Woven in dreams where joy is spread.

The cosmos sings a lullaby sweet,
In dazzling patterns, our spirits meet.
With every twinkle, stories unfold,
In this festival, our hearts are bold.

Galaxies swirl in a dance of grace,
Together we find our sacred space.
Hand in hand, we light the way,
In celestial fires, we laugh and play.

So delve into this cosmic stream,
Where every moment, a shared dream.
Under the stars, we'll always know,
In festive hearts, our love will grow.

Lullabies from Celestial Realms

In the night, the stars do play,
Whispers soft, in moonlit sway.
Melodies from skies above,
Carried here on wings of love.

Floating dreams in twilight's grace,
Every heart finds its own space.
Lullabies of cosmic cheer,
Sing to all who gather near.

Dancing lights in joyous flight,
Illuminating the quiet night.
With each note, the heavens sing,
Embrace the joy that starlight brings.

So let us gather, side by side,
In this festive, radiant tide.
With lullabies that never cease,
May our spirits find their peace.

A Glimpse through the Ether

In realms where laughter fills the air,
Ethereal voices dance without a care.
Glimmers of joy twinkle and shine,
In this moment, all hearts align.

The fabric of dreams beautifully spun,
Every soul joins in the fun.
Winds of fate carry us near,
Through the ether, full of cheer.

Bright colors swirl in joyful beams,
Painting the landscape of our dreams.
With every breath, we celebrate,
Boundless joy on our hearts we skate.

Let laughter echo through the night,
Filling our spirits with pure delight.
In this realm, where love is wide,
Together we shall joyously glide.

Beyond the Celestial Veil

Through the veil, the stardust glows,
Whispers of joy in gentle flows.
Cosmic secrets start to weave,
In every heart, they brightly cleave.

Illuminated laughter rings,
In this moment, our spirits sing.
Beyond horizons, wild and free,
Is where we find our harmony.

Each twinkling star a guiding hand,
Inviting us to dream and stand.
In this space, where hopes unite,
We celebrate beneath the light.

So dance with me, in pure delight,
Beneath the canvas of the night.
In cosmic joy, we intertwine,
As starlit souls, forever shine.

Stardust Beneath Our Feet

Beneath our feet, the stardust lies,
A sprinkle of magic under the skies.
In every step, we feel the grace,
Of ancient tales time can't erase.

With every heartbeat, a spark ignites,
Turning the mundane into delights.
Holding hands, we wander free,
In this festivity of harmony.

The air is thick with dreams unbound,
In the laughter, joy resounds.
Let opportunities lift us high,
As we reach for wishes in the sky.

Together, we'll dance on starlit ground,
In this moment, love will be found.
With every shimmer, our spirits soar,
In the light of dreams, forevermore.

The Skylark's Lament

In fields of gold, the lark does sing,
With joy that only spring can bring.
The sky above, so wide and bright,
Her notes dance freely, a pure delight.

Beneath the sun, where blossoms sway,
She paints the air in bright array.
A tapestry of chirps and glee,
Her voice a gift, for all to see.

Yet in her heart, a whisper low,
A longing for the winds to blow.
Through clouds and storms, she seeks the way,
To find the light where dreams can play.

With every note, the world expands,
The skylark dreams of distant lands.
Though joy fills eyes, a spark remains,
Of wistful songs and soft refrains.

Melodies from the Heavens

Stars twinkle bright in the velvet night,
Each one a song, a spark of light.
The universe hums a cosmic tune,
As planets sway beneath the moon.

With every note, the heavens beam,
A symphony beyond the dream.
Galaxies swirl, a vibrant dance,
Inviting all in a starry trance.

Listen closely to the cosmic call,
Voices echoed, a grand enthrall.
The air is thick with melodies sweet,
A festive air that can't be beat.

From distant worlds, the harmonies soar,
Uniting hearts forevermore.
A celebration of the night,
In every sound, pure bliss takes flight.

Celestial Cartographer's Journal

In parchment skies, the maps are drawn,
Of constellations kissing dawn.
Each line a path, all stars aligned,
A journey mapped, so well defined.

With compass poised and eyes aglow,
The cartographer scribes what they know.
Celestial wonders paint the way,
To hidden realms where dreamers play.

The ink dances, a festive swirl,
Sketching comets in a twirling whirl.
And through the cosmos, laughter rings,
As each new world a story brings.

Through nebulae of hues so bright,
Adventurers chase the hidden light.
In every stroke, a world reborn,
A joyous heart, no longer worn.

When Clouds Meet Light

When clouds embrace the golden glow,
A canvas waits for colors to show.
The sky ignites in radiant hues,
A festive moment that feels brand new.

Rain whispers softly, like a sweet song,
As sunlight breaks through, it won't be long.
Together they dance, in playful duet,
Creating beauty we won't forget.

Hope fills the air with a vibrant cheer,
As rainbows emerge, drawing us near.
Children laugh, with faces upturned,
While nature's wonders fill hearts that yearn.

So let the skies celebrate and sing,
With every cloud, a joyful wing.
For when clouds meet light, we're reminded anew,
That miracles bloom in every view.

Invitations from the Night

Stars twinkle like jewels in the sky,
Laughter spills softly, oh my!
Candles dance in a gentle breeze,
Whispers of joy float through the trees.

A tapestry of colors ignite,
With every moment, pure delight.
The moon smiles down with a silvery glow,
As friends gather 'round, hearts aglow.

Music weaves a magical thread,
Stories shared, and dreams fed.
In shadows, where secrets entwine,
The night wraps us in warmth divine.

So raise your glass, make a toast,
For joyful nights we cherish most.
With every heartbeat, let us sing,
To the festive joys that night shall bring.

Beyond the Arc of Nightfall

The sun dips low, painting the sky,
A canvas of dreams wishes to fly.
Stars appear, one by one,
The festive night has just begun.

Laughter rings through the twilight air,
As friends gather, joy to share.
Warm hearts meld under the moon's soft light,
Magic unfolds in the hush of night.

Flickering flames in the distance glow,
Encouraging spirits, let happiness flow.
With each whispered secret, hopes take flight,
Together we dance in the arms of night.

Raise your voice, join the refrain,
In this festive moment, there's no pain.
Beyond the arc where shadows rest,
We celebrate life, feeling blessed.

Face of the Immortal Sky

Beneath the stars, our laughter breaks,
A joyous cheer that the whole night wakes.
Under the celestial glow we stand,
With hopes and dreams, hand in hand.

The night unfolds, a velvet embrace,
Illuminating each glowing face.
Galaxies whisper their ancient lore,
As we come together, craving more.

Fires sparkle, crackling bright,
Guiding us through this blessed night.
Every wish tossed to the starry sea,
In this moment, we are truly free.

So join the circle, feel the delight,
In the face of the immortal sky tonight.
Sing and dance, let laughter ring,
For in this gathering, our hearts take wing.

When Horizons Whisper

When horizons whisper sweet secrets near,
The festive spirit dances, loud and clear.
Colors swirl in evening's embrace,
As laughter trails through this magical space.

Shadows play with the light on the ground,
In every heartbeat, our joys resound.
The air is thick with sweet melodies,
Under the charm of gentle breeze.

Gather 'round, let the stories unfold,
In this vibrant night, our hearts bold.
Cheers rise up as stars start to bloom,
In the friendship's warmth, we discard our gloom.

So let the night cradle us tight,
In the dreams we share, a beautiful sight.
When horizons whisper, let us be wise,
To cherish the moments 'neath open skies.

A Symphony Above

Stars twinkle like notes in the night,
Gather 'round, let spirits take flight.
The moon sings softly in silver hues,
While laughter dances in the warm evening zeus.

Fireflies twirl in a sparkling waltz,
Nature's orchestra plays without faults.
Joy resonating in the cool night air,
Together, we breathe music everywhere.

Beneath a tapestry of cosmic delight,
Every heartbeat echoes with sheer light.
In this vibrant gathering of fate,
A symphony unfolds, we celebrate.

Celestial Threads of Fate

Among the stars, our dreams entwine,
Celestial threads weave stories divine.
Each twinkling light a wish set free,
Binding us together, you and me.

The universe hums a joyous refrain,
With every heartbeat, there is gain.
In this mosaic of shimmering light,
We dance beneath the canvas so bright.

Galaxies swirl in a painted embrace,
Time stands still in this sacred space.
With every twirl, our spirits combine,
In this festival of love, pure and fine.

Unwritten Tales in the Firmament

Under the sky, stories reside,
Whispers of joy on the cosmic tide.
Unwritten tales in the vast expanse,
Inviting us all to join in the dance.

Each constellation a doorway to dreams,
Where laughter and light form radiant beams.
In this festive realm, hope finds its way,
As stardust swirls in joyful display.

Gathered beneath the celestial dome,
Together, we forge our stories at home.
With hearts wide open, we write our fate,
In unwritten tales that forever await.

Journey through the Nebula's Heart

In the cosmic cradle, we set our sails,
Through nebula's heart, where magic prevails.
With colors ablaze in the velvet night,
We journey along with pure delight.

Stars beckon brightly, they lead us on,
Through shimmering clouds till the break of dawn.
Every moment sparkles like fresh morning dew,
In this festival of dreams, just me and you.

Floating on wisps of the universe's art,
We sketch our adventures in cosmic chart.
In this radiant voyage, we play our part,
Celebrating life from the nebula's heart.

Echoes of Dawn's Embrace

The sun peeks in with rays so bright,
Colors dance in morning light.
Joyful notes of laughter play,
Welcoming the brand new day.

Flowers bloom with fragrant cheer,
Whispers tell us spring is here.
Children run with hearts so free,
Chasing dreams by the old oak tree.

Breezes carry melodies sweet,
As friends gather where paths meet.
Festive spirits fill the air,
Love and joy are everywhere.

As shadows fade and day awakes,
Echoes of laughter the heart takes.
Hand in hand, through fields we roam,
In this moment, we are home.

When Stars Conspire

Underneath a blanket of night,
Stars above, a wondrous sight.
Twinkling dreams in the cool breeze,
Whispers shared among the trees.

Laughter sparkles like the stars,
Bringing joy both near and far.
The moon smiles with a silver glow,
As friends gather, hearts aglow.

Songs ring out, a gentle tune,
Dancing shadows 'neath the moon.
With every note, our spirits rise,
In this magic, love never dies.

When stars align and wishes soar,
We find the meaning at our core.
In the night, we will conspire,
To keep our dreams forever higher.

A Tapestry of Clouds

In the sky, a canvas bright,
Clouds weave stories of pure delight.
Colors swirl in a playful dance,
Inviting hearts to take a chance.

Children laugh with purest glee,
Pointing out what they can see.
Whimsical shapes float on high,
Stitched by dreams that never die.

Picnics spread on soft green grass,
As moments like these quickly pass.
Lemonade and the warm sun's glow,
Together we let our spirits flow.

As shadows stretch and daylight fades,
The tapestry of joy cascades.
In every hue, in every sigh,
A reminder of how we fly.

Chasing the Horizon's Glow

As daylight breaks with golden gleam,
We set our sights on the horizon's dream.
With laughter echoing in the air,
A promise shared, a festive flair.

Every step a dance, a thrilling chase,
Finding joy in the open space.
Hand in hand, with spirits bright,
We venture forth, hearts taking flight.

Sunshine smiles as the clouds drift by,
Radiant colors paint the sky.
In the breeze, our worries cease,
This festive spirit, our hearts' release.

As the sun bows in evening's glow,
We treasure each moment, letting love flow.
In every sunset, stories unfold,
Chasing horizons, together we're bold.

The Unfolding of Cosmic Dreams

Under starlit skies we dance,
Whispers of magic in a glance.
Galaxies twirl, hearts take flight,
In the cosmic glow of the night.

Laughter rings like a silver chime,
Together we weave through space and time.
Each star a wish, a dream in bloom,
Filling the universe with sweet perfume.

With cosmic laughter, our spirits meet,
As meteors shimmer in joyous beat.
Hands held high, we celebrate,
The wonders of this endless fate.

Drifting through realms, in colors bright,
Under the moon's enchanting light.
In the tapestry of cosmic tunes,
We soar like dreams on magic dunes.

Colors of the Cosmic Canvas

Painting skies with hues divine,
As we gather, souls intertwine.
Crimson, azure, and golden rays,
Light up our hearts in wondrous ways.

Banners of joy in the evening air,
Swaying gently without a care.
In every color, every smile,
We find our joy, if just for a while.

Celestial hues of laughter bright,
Sprinkling dreams like stars at night.
Together we craft this vibrant guise,
In the boundless glow of cosmic skies.

As hearts unite in a joyful whirl,
The universe dances, unfurls.
With every stroke, our spirits rise,
In the colors of love that never dies.

The Interstellar Invitation

Come join the stars in playful cheer,
As laughter echoes, drawing near.
In cosmic corners, dreams take form,
A gathering where spirits warm.

Each twinkling light a call to play,
In the Milky Way, where wishes sway.
With open hearts, let's glide along,
In harmony, our voices strong.

Friendships bloom like flowers bright,
Under constellations shining light.
An interstellar embrace, so true,
With every heartbeat, I find you.

So take my hand, let's drift afar,
Through cosmic realms, where wonders are.
An invitation to dream and soar,
In this universe, forever more.

Hushed Wishes in the Atmosphere

In the quiet of the evening glow,
Whispers of wishes begin to flow.
Stars align as hearts unfold,
Secrets of dreams in silence told.

Velvet skies cradle hopes so high,
As we watch the night whisper by.
Under the moon's gentle sigh,
We catch hushed wishes that float and fly.

Each flicker of light, a wish released,
In the soft embrace, our joys increased.
Together we breathe in the gentle air,
A tapestry woven with love and care.

In this serene moment, we find delight,
As whispers of peace dance through the night.
With every promise, our spirits cheer,
Hushed wishes echo, forever near.

In the Grasp of Day's Resurgence

Golden rays cascade, bright and bold,
Laughter dances through the vibrant fold.
Joyful hearts embrace the sun's warm light,
As shadows fade, all seems pure and right.

Flowers bloom in colors, bold and bright,
Birds sing sweetly, lifting spirits high.
Together we unite in joyful cheer,
In this embrace of day, no room for fear.

The sky adorned with hues that sparkle clear,
With every whisper, memories come near.
We gather close, our souls entwined in glee,
In the grasp of day, we are all free.

So let us dance beneath this blazing glow,
And share our dreams where love and laughter flow.
In the rise of day, let our spirits soar,
A festive gathering forevermore.

Timeless Echoes of Airborne Wishes

Balloons ascend, dancing with the breeze,
Our hopes and dreams are carried with such ease.
Laughter rings and fills the joyous air,
In every heartbeat, there's a pulse of care.

Candles flicker, casting playful light,
Whispers of wishes float into the night.
Love surrounds us like a warm embrace,
In timeless echoes, we find our grace.

Children play beneath the starry sky,
Their laughter mingling with the moon's soft sigh.
A tapestry of colors lights the scene,
In our festive hearts, we know what it means.

So let your dreams take flight in joyous spark,
Let the night echo with love's sweet remark.
Together we'll weave memories anew,
In timeless echoes, our spirits break through.

Whispers of Celestial Voices

Stars ignite the evening with their glow,
A symphony of night, soft and low.
Celestial whispers fill the night air,
Invitations to a dance, a joyous flair.

The moon smiles down on all gathered near,
Enveloping us in love, dispelling fear.
As laughter weaves through every little sigh,
In this night of wonders, we learn to fly.

With every twinkle, hearts begin to soar,
The music flows, calling us to explore.
We twirl beneath the sky of endless dreams,
In the warmth of night, everything redeems.

So let our laughter echo, rich and bright,
In whispers of voices that guide us tonight.
Together we'll embrace this cosmic chance,
As festive joy leads us in a dance.

Beneath the Infinite Canopy

Beneath the stars, we gather hand in hand,
The universe unfolds, a magic land.
With every heartbeat, joy takes its flight,
In the canopy of wonder, pure delight.

Laughter mingles with the gentle breeze,
As wishes carry forth with such sweet ease.
Together we paint dreams in colors bright,
In this late hour, everything feels right.

The world alive with stories yet to tell,
In unity, we weave our festive spell.
Moments captured, held in time's sweet clasp,
Underneath the sky, life's joys we grasp.

So raise a glass to every soul we meet,
To the bonds we share, eternally sweet.
Beneath this infinite canopy, we see,
In love and laughter, we'll always be free.

The Language of Falling Stars

In the night where wishes gleam,
Falling stars weave vibrant dreams,
Laughter dances on the breeze,
Joyful hearts are sure to seize.

Candles flicker, warm and bright,
Shadows twirl in soft moonlight,
Whispers shared 'neath starry skies,
Hope ignites as spirits rise.

Echoes of a cheerful tune,
Colors splash like bright festoons,
Gathered friends with laughter near,
Celebrate the joys we cheer.

Sweet confetti in the air,
Every heart is light and rare,
In this fest, we all belong,
Falling stars, our hearts' own song.

Where Dreams Touch the Firmament

Underneath the vast expanse,
Dreamers slip into a trance,
Laughter bubbles, spirits soar,
Every heart feels love's encore.

Balloons rise in colors bright,
Chasing echoes of delight,
From the earth to starry heights,
Shadows dance in twinkling lights.

Voices blend in soft embrace,
Time dissolves in this sweet space,
Where the magic fills the air,
Dreams reach out with gentle care.

Every glance, a shimmering glow,
A tapestry of joy will flow,
Grateful hearts, and hands entwined,
In this night, pure love we find.

Celestial Serenade

Silver moons and golden beams,
Sing a song of joyous dreams,
Stars align in sweet array,
Guiding us in dance and play.

Laughter echoes through the night,
Hearts adorned in purest light,
Every note a blissful cheer,
As we hold our loved ones near.

Swaying under cosmic skies,
Magic sparkles in our eyes,
Melodies of life's embrace,
In this moment, find our place.

Together in this grand ballet,
Where celestial rhythms sway,
In the serenade, we glow,
Festive hearts in joyful flow.

In the Arms of Endless Above

Twinkling lights like sugarstars,
Wrap us in their world from far,
Winds of laughter softly play,
In this night, we dream away.

Crisp nights warm with fire's glow,
Gathering friends, spirits flow,
Every smile a cherished gift,
In this magic, hearts will lift.

Bubbles rise with wishes true,
Sharing dreams with skies of blue,
In the arms of endless above,
We find strength in joy and love.

Let us dance till morning light,
In the symphony of night,
Every moment feels so right,
In this realm of pure delight.

Whispering Horizons

Colors dance in twilight's glow,
Laughter spills where breezes flow.
Stars awaken, eager to gleam,
Night unfolds like a joyful dream.

Bonfires crackle, sparks in flight,
Voices echo through the night.
Hands entwined, we sway and sing,
Hearts alight with warmth of spring.

Cups raised high in cheerful cheer,
Memories made, friends gathered near.
In this moment, time stands still,
The joy of life our hearts will fill.

Underneath the moonlit skies,
Hope ignites as laughter flies.
Together we embrace the night,
In whispers soft, our spirits bright.

Beneath Celestial Arches

Beneath the arches, stars parade,
A tapestry of dreams displayed.
Flickering flames that twist and turn,
In their light, our spirits burn.

Gaily clad, we dance and sway,
Every heart resounds, hooray!
Joyful voices fill the air,
With every note, our burdens spare.

Glimmering lanterns float above,
Guiding us with light and love.
In this realm of pure delight,
Laughter echoes through the night.

Let the world around us fade,
In this bliss, our lives cascade.
With every toast and every tune,
We celebrate beneath the moon.

Echoes of the Infinite Blue

Ocean whispers kiss the sand,
Hope and joy go hand in hand.
Waves of laughter spill and flow,
Carried on the breeze so slow.

Surf and sun, the colors gleam,
Life unfolds like a radiant dream.
Children giggle, and seagulls play,
In this magic, we drift away.

Shells and treasures scatter wide,
Nature's bounty, our joyful guide.
With every wave, new tales arise,
In this place, our spirit flies.

As the sunset paints the sky,
Together under pinks and high,
We'll cherish moments, bright and true,
In the echoes of the infinite blue.

Dreaming in Ethereal Light

In fields aglow with silver beams,
Whispers carry our ancient dreams.
Kaleidoscope of colors bright,
We dance beneath the ethereal light.

Fireflies twinkle, a dazzling show,
Chasing shadows, they ebb and flow.
Mirth and music fill the air,
In every note, our souls laid bare.

With open hearts, we twirl and spin,
Welcome the night, let joy begin.
An orchestra of laughter rings,
In this celebration, love takes wings.

As stars entwine with stories told,
Gathered close, our spirits bold.
In dreams of light, we find our flight,
Forever bound, in festive night.

Night's Call to the Lost

Stars twinkle bright in the velvet sky,
Echoes of laughter drift softly by.
Waves of joy in the cool, crisp air,
Whispers of magic, everywhere.

Fireflies dance in a shimmering line,
Illuminating the paths we entwine.
Under the moon's gentle, watchful eye,
Hearts reawaken, as spirits fly.

Lively tunes wrap around the night,
Filling our souls with pure delight.
Each note a story, rich and bold,
A tapestry of dreams, brightly woven gold.

Celebrate life as the music swells,
Mysteries hidden, yet the heart tells.
Together we stand, hand in hand,
Bound by the rhythm of a merry band.

Resounding in the Heavens

Beneath the vault of shimmering stars,
Voices rise like fireworks from afar.
Laughter resounds, a sacred song,
In the warmth of friendship, we belong.

Each moment a treasure, sparkling and new,
Glances exchanged, a festive hue.
Candles flicker in the evening breeze,
Promising joy as hearts find ease.

Colors burst forth in a radiant show,
Dance of colors that swirl and glow.
Hearts beat as one, under the moon,
Echoing laughter, a joyous tune.

The night grows old, yet spirits stay bright,
Wrapped in the love, a beautiful sight.
We share this magic, one and the same,
Together we play in life's merry game.

Beneath the Veil of Dreams

In twilight's embrace, we gather in cheer,
Bright visions unfold, drawing us near.
With each whispered wish, the stars align,
A tapestry woven with hope and shine.

Moonbeams flicker on laughter's wings,
Adventure awaits, oh, the joy it brings!
Mysteries linger in the soft night air,
As dreams take flight, unbound and rare.

Under the starlight, we share our fate,
A dance of souls in an endless state.
Hands intertwined, we step into bliss,
Moments like these, we treasure and kiss.

With each heartbeat, the night sings sweet,
Rhythms of love, a melodic treat.
Together we rise, beneath the moon's gaze,
Igniting our spirits in a radiant blaze.

The Heartbeat of Distant Worlds

In an endless night where wonders spark,
Dreams of adventure ignite the dark.
Stars shimmer bright like secrets untold,
The heart of the universe, vibrant and bold.

We gather as one, beneath cosmic skies,
With twinkling eyes and joyous sighs.
Each laugh is a wish sent forth on a breeze,
Connecting our hearts, like the rustling leaves.

Colors spill out from the heavens above,
As constellations whisper of hope and love.
We dance upon stardust, twirling in glee,
Celebrating life, wild and free.

The night blooms alive with jubilant sound,
A symphony crafted from magic found.
Together, we'll dream of worlds far and wide,
Bound by the joy that we carry inside.

An Ode to Endless Heights

Up we soar on wings of cheer,
The sky's embrace is drawing near.
Laughter rings through jeweled air,
In festive joy, we share and dare.

Mountains gleam with sunlight's glow,
Echoes of our hearts in flow.
With every step, our spirits rise,
Together we'll dance 'neath wide blue skies.

Every breeze a story told,
A tapestry of dreams unrolled.
In unity, let's chase the day,
With laughter leading all the way.

Raise your glass, let's toast this bliss,
In every moment, a vibrant kiss.
As endless heights unfold and shine,
We're woven in this joy divine.

Starlit Pathways

Beneath the stars, we stroll tonight,
Each twinkle spins a tale of light.
With every step, magic in sight,
Our hearts ablaze, the world feels right.

The moon, a puppet in the sky,
Watches over as we sigh.
In whispers soft, our hopes take flight,
Across the night, our spirits fly.

Candles flicker, shadows dance,
Inviting all to join the trance.
With laughter ringing, all entranced,
We celebrate this grand expanse.

In this moment, joy ignites,
Each starlit pathway leads to heights.
With friends beside, we clasp our hands,
Together we make endless plans.

Choreography of the Cosmos

Stars collide in cosmic dream,
Across the night, we softly beam.
Galaxies swirl, a vibrant theme,
In unity, we plot and scheme.

With every dance, new worlds arise,
Like fireflies, we light the skies.
A symphony of joyful sighs,
In this vast stage, our spirit flies.

Colors burst in jubilant hues,
In laughter, we find our muse.
The universe sings, no time to lose,
As we embrace this festive fuse.

With hearts aligned, we seize the night,
In every star, a spark of light.
Together we twirl, feel the delight,
In cosmos' dance, our souls take flight.

Over the Whispers of Twilight

As twilight falls, the sky ignites,
Cascading colors, pure delights.
Whispers linger, sweet and bright,
In the glow, everything feels right.

The golden hour, a tender kiss,
In its charm, we find our bliss.
Every moment, magic's spun,
With laughter shared, we become one.

Beneath the arch of evening's grace,
With joy we wear our festive face.
Stories shared, each tale a trace,
In twilight's arms, we find our place.

So let us dance on this fine line,
Where day meets night, and hopes align.
With hearts aglow, we'll intertwine,
In the whispers of twilight, divine.

The Embrace of Twilight's Breath

Candles flicker, shadows dance,
Laughter echoes, come take a chance.
Joy spills over like crimson wine,
In this moment, everything is divine.

Stars awaken, the night feels bright,
Embracing wonders in gentle twilight.
Hearts entwined under velvet skies,
Together we laugh, together we rise.

Magic weaves through the evening air,
Every glance a silent prayer.
With arms outstretched, we gather near,
In this embrace, nothing to fear.

Time stands still as the music plays,
In jubilant hues, we lose our ways.
Life's canvas painted in passion's glow,
In the twilight, our spirits grow.

Horizons that Linger

Banners sway in the warm, soft breeze,
With every heartbeat, we aim to please.
Colors burst as the sun dips low,
Embracing moments, letting joy flow.

Voices rise in a cheerful song,
In this gathering, we all belong.
Glimmers of laughter and twinkling eyes,
Underneath the vast, open skies.

Gifts of friendship are shared tonight,
As stars emerge, they shine so bright.
Each embrace is a treasure we hold,
Stories woven, forever told.

Food and laughter spread wide and far,
We dance together, each a shining star.
In the embrace of the night we sing,
Celebrating life and all it brings.

Skyward Whispers

The moonlight whispers, secrets sweet,
Inviting dreams where hearts can meet.
Beneath the glow of shimmering light,
We celebrate the magic of the night.

Soft melodies drift, the air alive,
In every moment, new hopes thrive.
With open arms, we greet the song,
In this festivity, where we belong.

Twirling skirts and laughter shared,
Every spirit lifted, everyone dared.
The stars are witnesses to our cheer,
In this skyward dance, we have no fear.

Together as one, we lift our voice,
In the night, we joyously rejoice.
With every note, our souls ignite,
In the embrace of this vibrant night.

The Palette of Twilight

The horizon glows in a vibrant hue,
Painting dreams in shades anew.
Each moment captured, alive with grace,
In this tapestry, we find our place.

Brushstrokes of laughter fill the air,
A canvas of moments, love to share.
Through bursts of colors, we find delight,
Each heartbeat echoes in the soft night.

Spirits soar like kites on high,
Underneath the vast, starlit sky.
Bonfire crackles, warmth surrounds,
In the heart of night, joy abounds.

As shadows blend with twilight's glow,
We dance in harmony, feeling the flow.
In the palette of life, we paint our dreams,
In this festive eve, nothing's as it seems.

Resonance of the Orbital Chords

The stars align in joyful tune,
As laughter swirls beneath the moon.
With melodies that softly wove,
We dance in light, embraced by love.

A symphony of colors bright,
Echoes in the cool, sweet night.
Each heartbeat sings, a vibrant wave,
In this embrace, we're bold and brave.

Floating dreams on gentle sighs,
As wishes soar to paint the skies.
The magic flows like sparkling streams,
We celebrate our shared, wild dreams.

So raise a glass to joy anew,
In every glance, a hidden hue.
Together rise, our spirits free,
Resonance in our harmony.

Kindred Spirits in the Firmament

Underneath the starlit glow,
We gather 'round for tales to flow.
With sparkling eyes and hearts so light,
We share our dreams on this fine night.

The universe whispers our names,
In this vast dance, we're never tamed.
With laughter lifting every soul,
In unity, we find our whole.

The gentle winds carry our cheer,
In every beat, our hopes appear.
We twirl and spin in time's embrace,
Kindred spirits in this sacred space.

An endless bond, our stars ignite,
In cosmic joy, we feel the light.
As constellations brightly gleam,
Together, we will chase our dream.

In Search of Celestial Whispers

We seek the soft, celestial sound,
In twilight hues, our voices bound.
With every note, the cosmos sighs,
Awakening the dreams that rise.

In gardens filled with moonlit grace,
We wander through this timeless space.
A melody ascends the air,
In whispered hopes, we cast our prayer.

The stars, like lanterns, guide our way,
As we dance through night and day.
Each turn reveals a secret hue,
In harmony, we find the true.

In search of light, our spirits soar,
Exploring realms forevermore.
We gather dreams like scattered seeds,
And in their bloom, we find our needs.

Flights of Ethereal Birds

On wings of joy, we take our flight,
Through skies adorned with pure delight.
With laughter trailing in the breeze,
We soar above the whispering trees.

Each flap a heartbeat, wild and free,
Together, we embrace the glee.
In every color, every tone,
The essence of our hearts is shown.

As sunbeams dance on golden seas,
We find our balance in the ease.
With feathery grace, we leave behind,
A world of worry, gently maligned.

In unity, our spirits rise,
We sketch our dreams across the skies.
With wings unfurled, we greet the dawn,
In flights of joy, our souls are drawn.

Portrait of Skyward Longing

Balloons drift high, colors bold,
Laughter erupts, stories unfold.
Under the sun, the world feels right,
We dance in joy, hearts taking flight.

Picnic blankets on grass so green,
A tapestry woven, a vibrant scene.
Children chase dreams, their giggles ring,
In every moment, pure joy we bring.

Fireflies twinkle as dusk draws near,
Whispers of hope in the evening cheer.
Stars awaken, the sky ignites,
Our spirits soar on magical nights.

Together we bask in this radiant glow,
Embracing the love that continues to grow.
With each heartbeat, our souls intertwine,
In this portrait of longing, your hand in mine.

Enigmas of the Celestial Sphere

Glistening orbs in the velvet deep,
Secrets of time, a cosmos to keep.
Moonlight dances, shadows entwine,
In the vast unknown, our dreams align.

Constellations weave tales of old,
Whispers of stardust, mysteries bold.
Galaxies swirl in a waltz so grand,
Connecting our hearts, a delicate strand.

Meteor showers paint the night sky,
Wishing on trails as they swiftly fly.
Infinite wonders beckon us near,
In the silent realm, our hopes appear.

With every glance, the heavens ignite,
A tapestry bright, a glorious sight.
We dance to the hymns of the universe,
In the enigmas above, our hearts immerse.

A Skylit Reverie

The dawn breaks gentle with pastel hues,
As sunlight spills, the world renews.
Clouds whisper soft, a lullaby sweet,
In the embrace of morn, our hearts meet.

Waves of laughter on city streets,
Joyous melodies in the rhythm of beats.
As colors blend in the canvas sky,
Together we revel, just you and I.

Kites soar high, chasing the breeze,
A symphony rises, we feel the ease.
With every smile, a wonder unveiled,
In this skylit realm, our hopes are sailed.

Twilight beckons, hues start to fade,
Yet in our hearts, the memories laid.
With hands entwined, we greet the night,
In this reverie, everything feels right.

Ascending into the Ethereal

On wings of dreams, we rise and glide,
Through the azure waves, side by side.
With laughter bright, we chase the sun,
In this fleeting moment, we become one.

The stars call out, a distant song,
As night unfolds, we dance along.
In the cosmic embrace, we lose our fears,
Floating on whispers, our joy appears.

Nebulas bloom in colors rare,
An ethereal glow fills the air.
Together we journey, hand in hand,
Toward the mysteries of this wondrous land.

As dawn approaches, we'll still believe,
In magic and wonder, in what we weave.
With hearts ablaze, we ascend with grace,
In this ethereal realm, we've found our place.

Dance of the Wandering Clouds

Fluffy dancers twirl and sway,
In the bright blue sky they play.
Whispers of joy in the breeze,
Carried along with such ease.

Sunlight glimmers, shadows flee,
Painted skies for all to see.
Children laughing, hearts so light,
Wandering clouds, a pure delight.

As they drift, a song they sing,
Nature's stage, it's spring's bright fling.
Festive spirits, love's embrace,
In this joyous, open space.

Each moment shared, a little cheer,
Underneath the sky so clear.
Let's dance along, hand in hand,
With the clouds, we'll make our stand.

Ascending into the Ethereal

On wings of dreams, we rise and glide,
Through the azure waves, side by side.
With laughter bright, we chase the sun,
In this fleeting moment, we become one.

The stars call out, a distant song,
As night unfolds, we dance along.
In the cosmic embrace, we lose our fears,
Floating on whispers, our joy appears.

Nebulas bloom in colors rare,
An ethereal glow fills the air.
Together we journey, hand in hand,
Toward the mysteries of this wondrous land.

As dawn approaches, we'll still believe,
In magic and wonder, in what we weave.
With hearts ablaze, we ascend with grace,
In this ethereal realm, we've found our place.

Dance of the Wandering Clouds

Fluffy dancers twirl and sway,
In the bright blue sky they play.
Whispers of joy in the breeze,
Carried along with such ease.

Sunlight glimmers, shadows flee,
Painted skies for all to see.
Children laughing, hearts so light,
Wandering clouds, a pure delight.

As they drift, a song they sing,
Nature's stage, it's spring's bright fling.
Festive spirits, love's embrace,
In this joyous, open space.

Each moment shared, a little cheer,
Underneath the sky so clear.
Let's dance along, hand in hand,
With the clouds, we'll make our stand.

When Stars Speak in Silence

Glittering jewels in the night,
Whispers of magic, soft and bright.
Every twinkle a secret told,
In the cosmos, dreams unfold.

Gathered wishes float on high,
Underneath the velvet sky.
Each heartbeat echoes with delight,
As stars converse in silent light.

Festive laughter fills the air,
Children gaze without a care.
In this stillness, joy is found,
With the stars, we are spellbound.

When darkness dances on the ground,
The shimmering tales, profound.
Hearts unite beneath the glow,
In this endless cosmic show.

A Tapestry of Dusk and Dawn

Threads of twilight weave the glow,
As day surrenders to night's flow.
Colors blend in soft embrace,
Time held still in this sacred space.

Golden rays and shadows tease,
A canvas painted with such ease.
Festival of light and dark,
Nature's masterpiece leaves a mark.

Laughter echoes, fires ignite,
Gathered together in the night.
Under stars, stories are spun,
A tapestry that has begun.

With every heartbeat, spirits soar,
In this moment, we want more.
Celebrate beneath the sky,
As dusk and dawn together fly.

Chasing the Celestial Drift

On the breeze, dreams take flight,
Chasing echoes of pure delight.
Galaxies twinkle in the night,
Guiding us with their soft light.

The moon dances, a silver gleam,
Whispering secrets to those who dream.
Beneath its glow, we twirl and spin,
Chasing the stars, let the fun begin.

Festival of hearts alive,
Under starlit skies, we thrive.
Hands entwined, we wander far,
Together, we are the brightest stars.

A cosmic journey, a joyous ride,
In this festive world, we abide.
Chasing dreams that spark and lift,
In the night, we find our gift.

Songs from Above

Twinkling lights dance in the sky,
Melodies of joy as they pass by.
Whispers of dreams ride the evening breeze,
Lifting our spirits like the tallest trees.

Laughter echoes through the night,
With every star, our hearts take flight.
Celestial choirs sing a sweet tune,
A celebration beneath the moon.

Fires crackle, warmth all around,
Happiness blooms in the joyous sound.
Here we gather, friends side by side,
United in love, our hearts open wide.

Under this vast and starlit dome,
We find our place, we feel at home.
With each note, we weave our dreams,
In this festive night, nothing's as it seems.

The Interview with the Cosmos

Stars align for questions profound,
Whispers of truth in silence found.
What secrets lie in the vast unknown?
A dance of galaxies where wonders are sown.

The moon speaks softly in glowing hues,
Casting its light as an ancient muse.
Each twinkle bright with stories untold,
In the cosmos' lap, our dreams unfold.

Eager we seek the answers we crave,
In this grand theater, we all are brave.
With laughter and hope, we share our plight,
Hands raised high, we reach for the light.

And when confessions drift on the breeze,
Every heart sways as it aims to please.
A festive aura blankets the night,
In the interview with stars so bright.

Odes to Starlit Aspirations

In the cradle of night, dreams take flight,
Crafted by wishes that burn so bright.
Stars become beacons, guiding the way,
Whispers of hope in a grand ballet.

Each shimmer a tale of hearts so bold,
Woven in silver, spun from the gold.
A tapestry vast, where visions align,
Festive allure in the moon's design.

We celebrate boldly, the paths that we tread,
With laughter and joy, by dreams we are led.
In this cosmic dance, we find our place,
A vast universe filled with warm embrace.

Ode to the starlight that guides our way,
Filling our hearts on this magical day.
We raise our voices, let our spirits soar,
In a symphony of dreams, forevermore.

When Night Falls Softly

When night falls softly, the world awakes,
With stars above in a delicate flake.
Laughter and music fill the air,
In this festival of joy, we have our share.

Candles flicker in rhythmic delight,
Casting warm shadows in the cool twilight.
Folk tales linger, stories unfold,
In the heart of the night, life is retold.

Together we gather, hearts intertwined,
In each other's presence, peace we find.
With smile and cheer, we toast the night,
Dancing like fireflies, spirits in flight.

A feast of wonders beneath the stars,
Our hearts beat wild, unbound by bars.
When night falls softly, we celebrate free,
In a tapestry woven of joy and glee.

Echoing Songs in the High Blue

Beneath the sky so wide, so bright,
Joy dances in the morning light.
Voices lift, a harmonious cheer,
Every moment, the world feels near.

Colors burst in laughter's embrace,
With every smile, a joyful trace.
Songs of hope swirl in the air,
Echoing dreams, a love to share.

Flutes and bells play a soft tune,
As children play beneath the moon.
Laughter rings through every street,
In this festive spell, hearts do meet.

With open arms, we greet the day,
In the magic we find our way.
Together we sing the same song,
In the echoes where we belong.

Visions from the Starlit Beyond

In the velvet night, stars gleam bright,
Whispers of dreams take their flight.
Cosmic tales the heavens share,
With twinkling lights, we breathe the air.

Gathered close, we watch in awe,
The universe reveals its law.
Galaxies swirl in a stunning dance,
Inviting all souls to take a chance.

Radiant wishes drift like leaves,
In our hearts, the hope never leaves.
From distant realms, we feel the spark,
Guided by light through the dark.

With each blink, new visions arise,
Painting our dreams across the skies.
Hand in hand, we laugh and sway,
In the magic of this starlit play.

The Vibrant Portrait of Dusk

As daylight fades, colors ignite,
A canvas of hues in soft twilight.
Orange and pink blush the skies,
In this moment, the spirit flies.

Sculpted shadows stretch and sway,
The world wears a festive array.
Nature holds its breath in peace,
While beauty wraps our hearts in fleece.

Candles flicker in welcoming glow,
As laughter dances in the flow.
Friends gather close to share their tales,
Woven in joy, the spirit sails.

On this canvas, life's moments blend,
In vibrant strokes, joys never end.
Celebrating the twilight's grace,
In dusk's embrace, we find our place.

Atlas of the Spirit's Journey

With every step, we dance and twirl,
Embracing the magic of the world.
Paths lined with laughter, joy to find,
In the melody of hearts intertwined.

Mountains rise, their peaks aglow,
Whispers of wonder in breezes flow.
Journeys shared with friends so dear,
In every moment, love draws near.

Rivers shimmer as stories unfold,
Legacies written in hearts of gold.
Together, we sail on dreams so wide,
With every heartbeat, a festive guide.

In this atlas, let us chart our fate,
With spirits soaring, we celebrate.
Every laugh, every tear we weave,
In the tapestry of dreams we believe.

www.ingramcontent.com/pod-product-compliance
Ingram Content Group UK Ltd.
Pitfield, Milton Keynes, MK11 3LW, UK
UKHW021115181224
452675UK00023B/1247